THIS BOOK BELONGS TO:

_____

HELLO!

THANK YOU SO MUCH FOR PURCHASING MY BOOK! BEFORE YOU BEGIN YOUR COLORING ADVENTURE, PLEASE TAKE A MOMENT TO READ THIS:

PAPER QUALITY

THE PAPER USED BY AMAZON IS PERFECT FOR COLORING WITH COLORED PENCILS AND ALCOHOL-BASED MARKERS. TO PREVENT ANY BLEED-THROUGH AND PROTECT THE NEXT PAGE, PLACE A BLANK SHEET OF THICKER PAPER BEHIND THE ONE YOU'RE WORKING ON.

CONNECT WITH ME!

IF YOU HAVE ANY QUESTIONS OR CONCERNS, YOU CAN CONTACT ME AT TEACHINGBYJACCY.COM/CONTACT-US

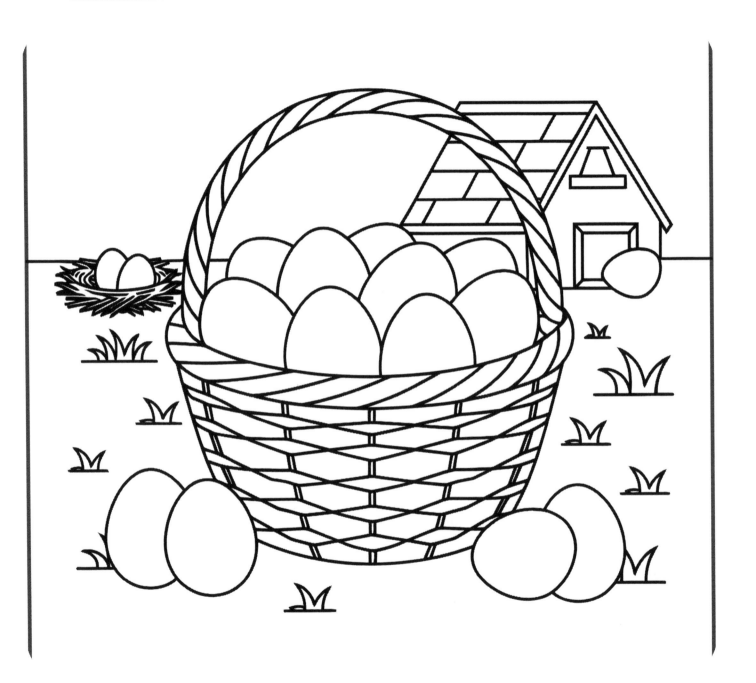

Made in the USA
Columbia, SC
19 December 2024

49909976R00057